SILENT TALKING

My Kundalini Nightmare

My Memoir of Being Supernaturally Forced to Service: Channeling Entities in an Occult Sex Cult

Adria Chalfin

Copyright © 2025

Adria Chalfin

Revised Edition

All rights reserved.

ISBN: 9780997848782 6

DEDICATION

This memoir is dedicated to life's journey and our courage to pull through and succeed.

CONTENTS

1 FROM THE HEART AND LIFE OF THE AUTHOR AND ARTIST - Pg 1

2 HOW IT ALL BEGAN - Pg 3

3 THE LOSS OF SELF - Pg 11

4 THE HOLE IN THE SOLE - Pg 15

5 CLAUSTROPHOBIC TERROR - Pg 19

6 SEXUALLY REVERSED AND USED - Pg 21

7 AN ENTITY SEX CULT? - Pg 26

8 FIGHTING FOR THE LIFE OF THE ABUSER - Pg 29

9 TOTAL CONFUSION - Pg 32

10 ACCELLERATING FORWARD - Pg 50

11 SILENCE AND TOTALLY ALONE - Pg 54

Silent Talking: My Kundalini Nightmare

'STOIC-SILENT TALKING' (when the words stop coming- physically & emotionally)

Silent Talking: My Kundalini Nightmare

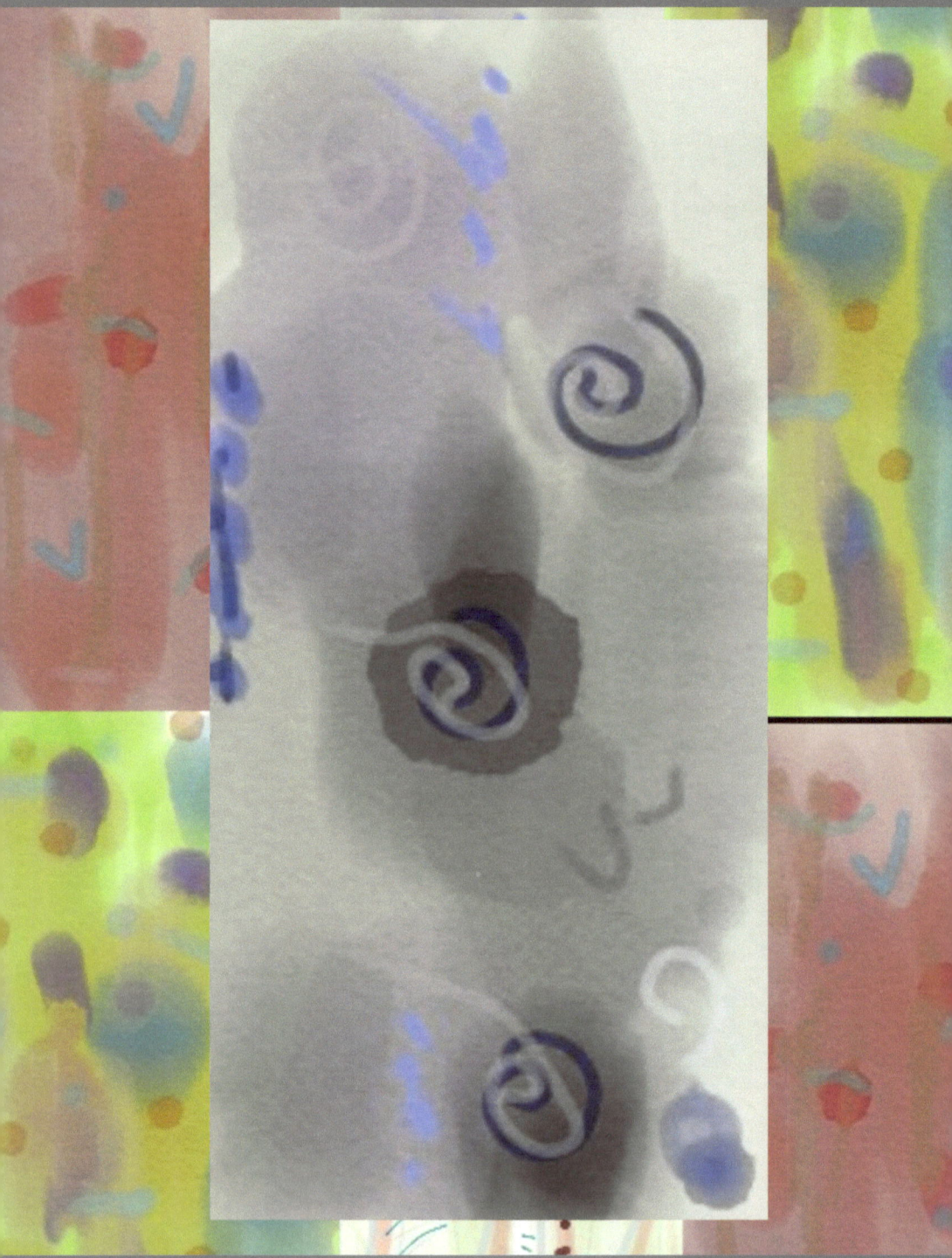

'Falling With Grace'

1

FROM THE HEART AND LIFE OF THE AUTHOR AND ARTIST

Life is hard. Mine being at the extreme of super hard. I publish this book at the incredible mark of my tenth straight year absolutely alone. How can this happen to anyone you may ask? I guess time for recovery and unbelievable circumstances.

I myself fear that thirty years of isolated trauma—that I haven't been able to share—and I was so deeply and impossibly wounded from—has created for me a state of unsolvable isolation inside. No one—let alone intimately—seems to have the key to unlock me out of remaining alone. On this very day in January 2024—(ten years later) it's pouring forth a little on these pages. I am truly too pained to lay out thirty years of story—but I am hoping that this eruption can help you face your life—as it is a part of my healing to face mine.

Silent Talking: My Kundalini Nightmare

'Life Waterfall'

How It All Began -

The Kundalini Event Trigger

It begins I am supposing because unknowingly to myself back then, I have a natural givers nature of selfless inclination. It ends with the giving up of life as I knew it. A pursued dream career I had trained for since five years old and achieved my first young adult successes at—was just instantly dropped. My sexual dreams of marrying in a heterosexual relationship were just suddenly abandoned. Not necessarily by my own choice, but by the result of being overwhelmingly emotionally manipulated and persuaded, I am supposing. And yes, I blame myself looking back, for having such a disposition that was so susceptible. Where was my fight or my flight response to the given situation? It was missing entirely. Instead of continuing on the path to the fruition of all my hard work and all my dreams—swiftly life instead became in totality the experience of being in the perpetual presence of what I realize now to be a psychotic 'takers' narcissistic reality. I am referencing a woman born female and happily so. She prided in the glory of her womanhood and feminine power—relishing in her soul's superiority as she perceived it. This manifested in her behavior to the point of down right refusing ever to make a movement sexually or socially that would suggest masculinity, as in the act of actually 'fucking' another woman. This would taint the purity of her living her truth. And yes, even if she dared to force a female friendship into a full out lesbian relationship with another woman! She had zero comprehension that the woman was a woman. She seemed to live in the illusion that the woman was a man, and therefore sex was complete after she was given it, achieving her feminine vaginal orgasmic glory. I learned this about her the hard way. I had no thought or concerns about it at all in the beginning because this was just a friendship, and that was all I wanted. I wanted men. (I am a woman—happily so, and jive heterosexually.) Her tactics were so brilliant that I became so immersed in the experience of knowing her—I lost perspective on my own identity completely. It's like feeling the attack of an endless stream of verbal bullets called friendship to sexual experiment one time thing, to full blown relationship trap and not recognizing that they were bullets that landed you there, but perceiving them as superior wisdom and truths. I became immersed in the experience of trying to succeed at becoming the opposite sexual orientation of my nature. I became immersed in her pressure for me to become a lesbian, for the sake of pleasing her lust for pleasure. I had no idea at the time she was pressuring me or that she was lusting even. It was underneath the surface of a regular platonic 'girls' friendship. I had no idea her eyes were on me in this way, that I was her target. I see now she saw in me an individual that could be groomed to be a slave for her. She was a severely controlling individual that demanded to be friends and then evolved to demand from me 'forever'. I had entered her dictatorship without any awareness of that fact or desire to do so. I realize now she wanted me to be the DOM to her, but without the costumes or kinky stuff—which is why I didn't recognize what was really going on. She was '*DOMing*' me into becoming the DOM for her. It was a twisted scenario of contradiction. She had the dominating controlling personality, not me at all! I never wanted to become the Dom or I should say MAN in the sexual dynamic. I never wanted to be with her sexually at all. I got caught up in her upset at me for not doing it correctly and lost sight of the fact that I never wanted it in the first place! I see only now that she was a master at emotional manipulation and cruel selfish control. Start with one-sided sexual demands (only to be pleased by me but never to touch me), then take it way further with aspects like strict laws of OCD practices—including enduring physically painful rituals she demanded I follow.

People discuss being the victim of *'their own'* OCD thoughts, but never have I heard of someone forcing someone else to endure them and have them be painfully abusive. Some of the rituals she practiced but some she actually *'did'* to me, like clearing every pore on my face and back and chest with her fingernails. The sessions would go on for about an hour and it was nerve sting torture over and over—pore by pore. Especially when every couple days she would dig into all the pores that were still sore from the last 'clearing'. At the time I tried to tell myself that she had a higher purpose for doing this to me because she represented herself as a goddess. Now that I have learned about OCD, I am assessing otherwise. I am determining she was a sadist all the while playing victim to her own OCD thoughts—again a twisted contradiction. She never saw her OCD thoughts as a problem she needed help for, she saw them as purposeful spiritual necessary things she must do to protect (more on this later), and I believed in her. Another aspect of her emotional manipulative abilities to the point of mastery, was how she could put me down the rabbit hole of perpetual guilt tripping (more on this later as well). And this is really me only touching the surface about it all, and briefly gives you an idea of the kind of person I was in the presence of, during my nightmare event. Kundalini experiences are supposed to be spiritual awakenings—but mine became a spiritual nightmare.

Before it occurred, I realized that this unexpected relationship that entered my life unwished for and unfelt for, but cunningly coaxed into, had literally put me in a state of shock. This state of shock could have been the trigger that opened my third eye and manifested a psychic experience I wasn't choosing—but was possibly a trauma response instead. This result was not of spiritual benefit or awakening for me, but only benefitted the person who forced me there in the first place by traumatizing me. This will all be made clear a little later. A complete reality about-face had befell me knowing her. I was being gaslit with fury for absolutely everything, even as far as having personal dreams, worldly and sexual at all, before meeting her. The worst guilt was formed from her endless rages and disappointment in me, that I was not a virgin for her and she still was. I tried to appease this and help her upset, by setting her up with a boyfriend to have her own heterosexual experience. She wasn't too invested in succeeding and dropped trying after a couple of failed attempts. That left me in the guilt of her rages. '*How dare I*' was the crux of the matter. I could never escape or make up for this. I could never get my virginity back and give it to her. This onslaught of guilt inducement completely side tracked me from the point that I was heterosexual and wanted to be! I became the result of the blame that I had failed being true to her instead. When I said rabbit hole—I meant rabbit hole! It went so far that I even began to become ashamed of my heterosexuality entirely (which never changed inside). Devastated by her instilled guilt and living from that moment forth to please her, I had no comprehension at the time—that I was being martyred to live to suppress all my own feelings and sexual orientation. I had no comprehension because shortly in—I couldn't perceive my own feelings, wants or needs anymore. Her demands were harsh and succumbing to them became my default. For example, I accepted her no masturbation rule—even though she never planned to touch me. I was feeling deserving of that punishment to atone for the fact that I was no longer a virgin when I met her. My first boyfriend just wanted to devirginize a girlfriend as a bucket list and then they moved on. I would have married as a virgin had I been given the opportunity, but heterosexually. I was so destroyed by her rage at me, that I actually blamed myself and felt deserving of her punishment—not to be touched, never to have an orgasm again. In terms of sex, I tore myself apart inside if she wasn't happy with my performance in bed, and she was drastically demanding and harshly cruel about it. As an example, she wanted to have an orgasm from a spot in her back and would demand up to hours of work to get in the right place. She refused to tell me where the right place was and it always seemed to move from day to day. I of course was confused, my back was a back, not a sexual organ. But if

I finally got it right, there would be an undertone sigh I could barely make out, and I was free. This scenario repeated itself for years. Sex became an upset stomach to get through and perform. If I succeeded, I could calm down until the next time. I always dreaded my decision to try for a second vaginal orgasm. If it would fail, the unforgiveness and seething upset was unbearable.

By the way, as I had said before, this began as a friendship. She had a boyfriend at the time we met, (I was between boyfriends). I even observed them kissing at the work Christmas party—but oddly she spent that whole night talking to me instead. She spent a couple months trying to suggest guys at work I should approach to date. She knew I was heterosexual and had boyfriends in college. We had both just graduated from different schools and met during an internship in the arts, i.e. television production. She was an aspiring filmmaker/writer/director, and I had graduated in fine arts with a bachelor's degree in dance and choreography. I was a member of a dance company while I was interning at the cable tv station where we met. This was Los Angeles 1984.

Silent Talking: My Kundalini Nightmare

(Me) Contemporary Dance Solo

3
THE LOSS OF SELF

I unknowingly to my naive and sincere personhood until recently realized, had in fact, met my own personal *kryptonite in human form.

(*Kryptonite: that which can completely overwhelm you to the point of total destruction and targets just you, and only you as in the story of Super Man.)

I had agreed for a one night stand sort of thing in that girly kind of friend way—my fatal mistake for a lifetime. I started oddly to cry after I agreed, and expressed to her that it won't be just once and I will never have my dream of getting married (heterosexually). I was pouring tears—my instincts had come forward and I saw with insight what this 'once' sexual experience with a female friend would truly mean. I was suddenly and unexpectedly overwhelmed. She looked back at me blankly and said nothing. As tears poured down my face my soul froze—knowing but incapable of getting off the course. She proceeded to follow through with *'the plan'*. That manner of moving forward without a single hesitation or concern for my feelings seemed to cause me to drop them as fast as she did. I realize now that somehow I was already weakened and caught in her ability to destroy me.

Silent Talking: My Kundalini Nightmare

Silent Talking: My Kundalini Nightmare

That was me the *'morning after'*, before her rages and my channeling entities nightmare began. It was Mother's Day of all things, and we took both our mothers out together. That was her mother's martini that I was told to take a photo with. I don't drink. I had a soul stomach ache at that moment, that obviously didn't show—and never could have guessed this moment was about it for my life as I knew my life to be.

Silent Talking: My Kundalini Nightmare

'Broken'

4

A HOLE IN THE SOUL

It was oddly one sided, giving only on my part and then she contently falling asleep. I figured maybe later, but that was never going to be the case. I realized she was a master at reverse psychology all these years later. She would rant on how her mother would never let her finish a conversation without falling asleep first. It never dawned on me as I suffered for that injustice her mother did to her, that she was always falling asleep on me, and to get out of giving SEX. I can't imagine it took all these years to notice that! I say 'kryptonite' metaphorically speaking, because in addition to this entire personal trauma, as if that wasn't enough, (my reference to my life being super hard) a spiritual psychic phenomenon nightmare befell me with this individual as well.

After one of the moments of emotional slaughter, her intense anger pouring out at me for past boyfriends, when she read an old college journal of mine and realized, *I loved them*—suddenly out of the blue, I felt a hole was opening up in my soul. I screamed as it was happening and received no concern. I seemed to speak from a knowing place that startled me at the moment, "A hole is opening up in me. I don't think I can control whether good or bad comes through." Those were the last words I had control to speak through my own body. This was North Hollywood Los Angeles 1986. My soul was slammed to the back right side of my body and stuck there immobilized but completely conscious. Angel spirits she declared later as her children, began channeling through me as well as lovers with masculine oriented sexuality towards her. That's when the OCD pain rituals, such as being forced to hold-in 'bathroom' for twenty-four hours to protect them, began. I was no longer referenced as a person, I was now '*call*'. This is not the present use of the term 'channeling', where people say they channel someone like portraying them. This is the 1980's assessment when entities actually take you over. (You can reference Edgar Cayce - Clairvoyant and Shirley MacLaine - Actress and Author on the subject.) I had no choice, I was frozen. Each month or so I would break through and yell—"I am back here pinned inside myself, can't move or speak". Her response was to ignore me and lust for the next spirit call and then proceed to slap my face if my crying out interrupted and ruined the 'call'.

By the way, this all took place in an apartment she chose for us to move into after she had coxed me into a relationship. I never wanted to move in there—it felt eerie, filled with darkness and frightened me. But she loved it and we moved in. It was built back in the 1920's if I recall. It was one story attached to other units in a U shape and then there was a two story building built later on the same small property in the back. It had an art deco fountain, a stucco roof, and was painted a coral hue on the outside - with one bedroom, one bath, a claw tub, old hardwood floors and a gas furnace in the floor on the inside. It looked like old Hollywood and had creepy energy. It was torn down in the late 1990's and there is a modern apartment building there now. I was right never to move in there. 'There' is where my life was ruined. I gave in and let her have what she wanted.

Silent Talking: My Kundalini Nightmare

'Calming After Panic'

5

Claustrophobic Terror

I physically had no choice but to be of service. I felt so worthless from the guilt forming fury she gave me prior, that as I was paralyzed in the situation, I mentally justified my worth now to be as a servant to these higher beings. My life's dreams faded far from me as the brutality of losing my agency took front and center stage. The entities presence through me were large and stunning, and the 'angel children' had lovely voices. I was 'kryptonited' (realizing this now, looking back). I knew I could never refuse being of service to beings so much greater than I—even if I did gain control back of my body. I saw I could never fathom the possibility of living again —because that would mean I would be taking her only way to be with her angel children away from her. I couldn't venture towards that thought. Surely the spirit realm wouldn't have halted my life if there was another way. I was to be martyred for this cause. I felt hyperventilating claustrophobic terror that this was it for me, there would be no going back. I had to be a frozen immobilized observer, a vessel for spirit entities to live through me indefinitely. That was to be my purpose now and it was devastatingly chosen for me.

Silent Talking: My Kundalini Nightmare

'Total Fear'

6

SEXUALLY REVERSED AND USED

Please note, in regards to her entity soul lovers (the angel children were all girls), they were all men or identifiably concentrated masculine sexual energy. I was a feminine woman with this massive amount of mojo traveling through me. Even though I could perceive their kindness and sensitivity, I still had to gird all womanly feelings. I had to erase my existence alive in my own body. I felt I was reversed, turned inside out and actually wondered as the years progressed, if I wanted to be a man in my head, but realize now, never in my heart. Early on she always treated me like I was the guy in the relationship. She would get furious at me like I was the bad guy. It was like the pain I suffered from unlucky boyfriend choices before I ever met her, was now turned back at me. Now she was the woman hurt by the bad guy and that was now *me*. But I never betrayed her or treated her coldly or anything when I was with her before the channeling began. It was in all actuality, always about sexual performance, even from the entity-soul lovers. Her entity lovers were all men or identified as masculine as I was saying. She was hostile and bitchy about the fact that they were all men and I didn't have a penis. She blamed me.

This was another twisted contradiction. I lived the upset as if it were my fault that masculine energy entities were taking over a woman (me) to have sex with her. Sometimes in my mind I tried to 'will' my body to grow a penis just to solve the upset. Some years later I thought of having a sex change just to appease the situation, but thank god we had no money or health insurance so that never came to be. Oddly, no matter how furious she was, she never suggested it. I realize she must have known what I realize now, that I had to be of the most feminine energy (that which she declared she was) to become a channeler. That feminine energy receives and could receive the entities' *'calls'*, even though they were men for the sex sessions. The men entity lovers must have known that as well. Masculine energy repels and could never transmit. If I had changed my gender it may have all shut down. Hypothetically speaking, by this point it wasn't my penis she would have wanted without those men entities 'calling' and it would have been an absolute disaster for me. Even further than the disaster I was already living in! The sex sessions were through my body and because of that I felt responsible for everything. One of my most drastic troubles began early on. When the entity men would take over (by the way I could distinctly differentiate between them and even recognize their nuanced differences) they would begin making love to her as if they had a penis before switching to a hand job, cunnilingus or the dildo she named 'Man'. The lovers seemed to have no awareness that they were rubbing my vagina against her. 'Calls' usually transmitted much more clearly when they began clothed, and this contributed to the problem of the 'clothing to vagina rub'. If during the extreme sexual sessions I began to get close to *'coming'* from the unintentional rubbing, I would freak. Me interfering and experiencing a kind of superficial rubbing orgasm during her entity relationship sex—I could never live with the guilt of that. If one day I could talk again through my own body I could never live with that on my conscience, I would have to confess it. Her entire life was dedicated to 'her privacy' and I had no way to tell her I was consciously there during all of her sex sessions. I had to live with the stress of that guilt. I figured I may never survive her rages when the day came but adding this aspect to confess was not something I was going to allow. If I was about to experience this sexual side effect, I literally would cause a stop to the flow of the 'call' and pull back from the rubbing for a few seconds (until my cloth rubbing climax possibility was stopped) and then let the presence of the entity back to resume the lovemaking. Somehow that brief ten second pause would 'turn her off' even though the love making resumed. She would get all pissy and angry and it would take extreme extra effort from the man entity for her to climax. I knew I caused the interference every time but decided I couldn't live with letting myself experience that even more than causing the horror of disruption. Interestingly, this led to me discovering that I had a soul muscle that could contract to pause a 'caller's' transmission for a brief amount of time, even if I couldn't talk or move my own body yet. Please note that channeling is completely draining and exhausting for the channeler. I was expected to keep it up indefinitely. Most accounts of channelers explain that they knowingly consent to lending themselves and go unconscious when they are channeled through and the spirit entity embodies them. The spirit entity usually borrows their body for a brief amount of time to convey an important spiritual message they need relayed to the world or to perform a healing for someone who has come to the entity via the known channeler for a healing. The spirit guides-entities in this manner are recorded as being very careful not to drain the host person too far of their life force before they end the session. My experience was exactly the opposite. That was terrifying, but I still blamed myself that I failed if anything ever went wrong and she didn't 'love' the experience or end up sexually satisfied enough—even if perhaps I did not. I had to learn to let go of all wants, all feelings, all fears in a state of STOIC SILENCE.

Silent Talking: My Kundalini Nightmare

'Stoic'

7

An Entity Sex Cult?

The entities' presence and her newly found declarations overwhelmed me. She declared herself the 'Light of Truth'. Her angel children The Lights of Care, Sincerity, Love, Faith, Compassion and Hope. She named her masculine lovers as if they were the gods like of Atlantis or Ancient Greece or Rome. Boy was I in trouble now—how I must not fail! I must endure more tortuous face clearing sessions and hold in bowel movements and urine for twenty-four hours without falter and there's so much more. I must persevere to keep all 'calls' pure. These were the historic gods—the greats, but it began to feel like a spirit sex cult. I felt used and greatly abused and completely confused. I had no choice, their energies were too strong for me, but my soul was crying out. Crying out to return—to regain control. I was at odds with her will and the entities' wills and my souls will. In the present day I have realized that the psychic entrapment that forced me to serve her egomania I now see as her becoming a spirit cult leader and I was the only talent/ vessel for her reign. It was a spiritual sexual cult that formed through me with her as their leader in secret.

Silent Talking: My Kundalini Nightmare

As all this is occurring, one of the caller/ lovers is encouraging her to produce her movie, a Sci - Fi about facing your fears. I thought it was fantastic when she read it to me at the beginning of our friendship. Please note as the years passed I myself and 'callers' through me, sent the movie script and delivered it personally to studios and agents. There was no purchase, but suddenly Star Trek, a reality show and a movie all came out with 'facing your fears' themes. In fact it's totally old hat now. I at the time saw her as a victim again and felt awful for her. Now all these years later, I am realizing the impossible possibility that it was her justice. I almost can't even let myself believe it. I only saw her as a victim and suffered for all the injustices she experienced. I never could see what I am expressing to you now—in any way, shape or form. Remember, I felt like nothing to myself and deserved punishment. Part of the rope that bound me was the incredibly written movie. Little did I realize that I was the only one facing my fears.

'Stressed Out'

8

FIGHTING FOR THE LIFE OF THE ABUSER

Her movie deceived me that she was a great person like her writing. This has been one of my great life lessons. I have now had many experiences to see that a creator of great literature, art, etcetera, doesn't make a great or even good person. They actually as a pattern tend to be egomaniacs. I, as naive as I explained, never knew this. My father was a writer and a lovely spiritual seeker. His two screen plays were fantasy musicals for children and I loved them. He'd read and act/sing them to me as a child. He dedicated his life to social work to support us and died early from the pressure, with his screenplays unmade. See —that's sort of where I pick up the selfless and add to it my own.

Well, after years of canvasing it all started to come together. A known actress said 'yes' to being interested and that we could use her name to find a production company to fund the Sci-Fi film. A seasoned production designer was interested in beginning, while we were working on finding funding. This was a twenty-five million dollar sci-fi with vast special effects. It was 1990. It was thrilling, but unnerving because we didn't have the funding yet.

While in pre-production talks from home ((grandparents), and I am simultaneously still the 'call', her tooth breaks on popcorn and she proceeds to swallow her amalgam cavity filling that is filled with mercury. She takes ill and has to immediately cancel the project. She was twenty-nine by this time. She was twenty-two, I was twenty-one when all this started. A slow horrible, painful poisoning with symptoms for the next twenty-four years resulted. I felt so awful for her. I was desperate to save her and wished she went to the hospital. If only she would have had her stomach pumped, if only she would go to the dentist. Then I thought well, surely these entities would save her. The gnawing feeling in the pit of my stomach said something else, that I was the only one to cure her. All of this 'greatness' with me as her vessel, was something she ordained her 'privacy'. For her and only her. Her mercury poisoning symptoms now became her 'privacy' as well. I was the only one that was enlisted to serve her 'privacy' no matter in how many aspects it manifested. I and I alone must save her. She hid her health crises from everyone else completely.

Silent Talking: My Kundalini Nightmare

'I Don't Know'

9

TOTALLY CONFUSED

I now made it my next life mission to save her. I was isolated alone with her carrying on the 'calls' that weren't saving her before my very eyes. I got stronger to talk again after many years and when I would be allowed to return forward in my body for short periods, I would go to every health food store across the entire United States, reading every book and trying every possible cure. No cell phone or internet research was in existence yet. Back then the cell phone caused cancer and we stayed away due to her electromagnetic sensitivity as well. Each health program I tried would gain improvement for a few weeks and then every symptom would not only return, it would increase. Her mother was depositing funds for her to live on and was always broke. Sometimes we had only two dollars for two days. We drank sips from a quart sized container of half & half only, for the entire day. That was her choice for the best nutrition for two dollars. She wouldn't let me work even though I begged her, because my hands had to stay clean and holy to give sex to her. We had determined that the materials in dildos were probably exasperating her condition by increasing her immune system response, so it was rarely used until it was stopped altogether. As a note, I never could gel with the practice of 'dildo-ing' anyway. I never wished to have a penis and she forced the issue by demanded early on I go into a sex shop she drove me to and purchase one. This was in the pre-channeling days. Honestly, I wasn't very familiar with sex shop reality and that dildo scared me! Going in and buying it when I didn't want to, was a drastically sickening experience. Using it felt like poking someone with a foreign object dissociated from my attempt to love and care with feelings and the ability to give pleasure. If I tried to strap it on, it would always slip and never stay aligned with my movements. It might even plunge in the wrong direction and miss and even slip off my body. It was always an awkward fight to make it work and anything but caring lovemaking. It felt instead like I was raping—like how the gynecologist sticking metal in my vagina was a rape experience for myself. I was now the gynecologist trying to enact lovemaking with a violating tool. She responded to it when we tried so I continued sometimes, but it still felt like she was asking me to rape her. She would get furious with me that I was the one who couldn't work it right. I never mastered it at all. I think they design them much more functionally now, but I still would feel the same. Frankly, I was happy it was abandoned for the sake of her health.

I preferred giving to her exactly what I would want for myself, and that's how I handled it. It was used for some of her sex sessions, but rarely, and eventually stopped. Looking back, I wonder if my will in the matter did influence the 'calls' after all. It was never a first choice to grab the dildo. After all, I was there observing—with no choice not too! I would pang in upset if it was ever approached and used.

So back to the original subject, that sex was predominantly expressed with hands and lips. I could completely comprehend her logic that I must keep my hands holy, because she was. I was under her spell. Because I wasn't allowed to work and bring in a steady income, we only had enough money to buy the supplements, herbs, essential oils, cleansing and chelating heavy metal programs - when the funds were erratically deposited. This unnerved me completely. Her health was slowly but steadily taking downturns and as I mentioned before, when I would succeed at purchasing the next health program I had found, in the great hopes of her recovery, it would help for a few weeks and then backfire and her symptoms would worsen. I never gave up. I was always searching. By this time her skin was burning and we had to travel from town to town across the United States looking for places with less cell phone towers, they would electric shock her. This would be the year 2000, when cell phone towers were just beginning to pop - up all over the United States. We were literally racing to find a town anywhere that didn't yet have one. If she lived too close to the 'signal', she would experience electric shocks continuously. Her 'skin burning' refers to skin ulcers forming on her calves. It began as one in the early 1990's and the number increased as the years moved forward (more on that later). We rarely had money for even an economy motel so we stayed in the car mostly. Even if we were able to get a winter rental deal with her mother's help, we had to leave because the longer she stayed in one place, the more painful it became for her. Then a new aspect had developed during the time of continuous traveling. She would look up and point to the airplanes overhead and insist they were following her and intentionally dumping chemtrail chemicals on her. So we were always running from that as well. That was completely her own idea at the time, she called it 'dumping chemicals' and said they were after her to make her even sicker. This was years before the chemtrail conspiracy theories hit the internet. Remember the internet was just beginning. (Just to note, about a decade later she got her first cell phone, went to YouTube and found an entire group discussing chemtrails. She was thrilled and felt vindicated that she was right.)

Throughout the decades after channeling had begun as all this was transpiring, she began to have revelations that she recognized the men and angel children that were 'calling'. She identified them all as famous actresses and famous athletes in Hollywood. She was an avid watcher of people in Hollywood. Life with her was years of unfolding shock for me. When she would recognize one of the entities who 'called' her sporadically over the years, she would begin to follow their careers to the T. Why am I trapped to channel them if they are out there? I was totally confused. If you had just continued your pursuits as a filmmaker you would have met them, I would say to myself. OMG what was I forced to live for and forsake my life for? I will not be naming names, to protect myself. When I observed that they all had other lovers in the world my heart broke for her. I gained more strength over the years and began to tell her I didn't have the heart to see them break her heart like this, out there with girlfriends and wives and 'calling' and making love to her. And imagine her six girl-women angel children that she said didn't partake in sex, were out there married, divorced or dating men! She had identified them all as adult very famous actresses in Hollywood, all about our age, from our generation. I never had time to sort all this out because I was preoccupied with the intense guilt from blaming myself that somehow I was responsible, that my channeling ability was bad and that's why they couldn't remember their 'calls'. Obviously they weren't remembering their 'calls', I assessed. Was my channeling ability such a failure that I caused them all not to remember that they knew her, loved her and worshipped her daily? I was facing a new terror that they didn't remember a thing and it was all my fault. I couldn't bear this. They were all out there? The 'calls' from the entities that froze me and took me over were powerful and overwhelming. How could it be possible? Was it their higher selves and in the world they were asleep? My mind raced with endless possible deductions. Were they just out of body traveling and when they returned to their bodies they were doomed never to remember? Was it drugs? Was it a drug popular in celebrity circles that gave them these out of body sexual trips? Is this what I lost my entire life for? I was desperate inside and in despair.

Silent Talking: My Kundalini Nightmare

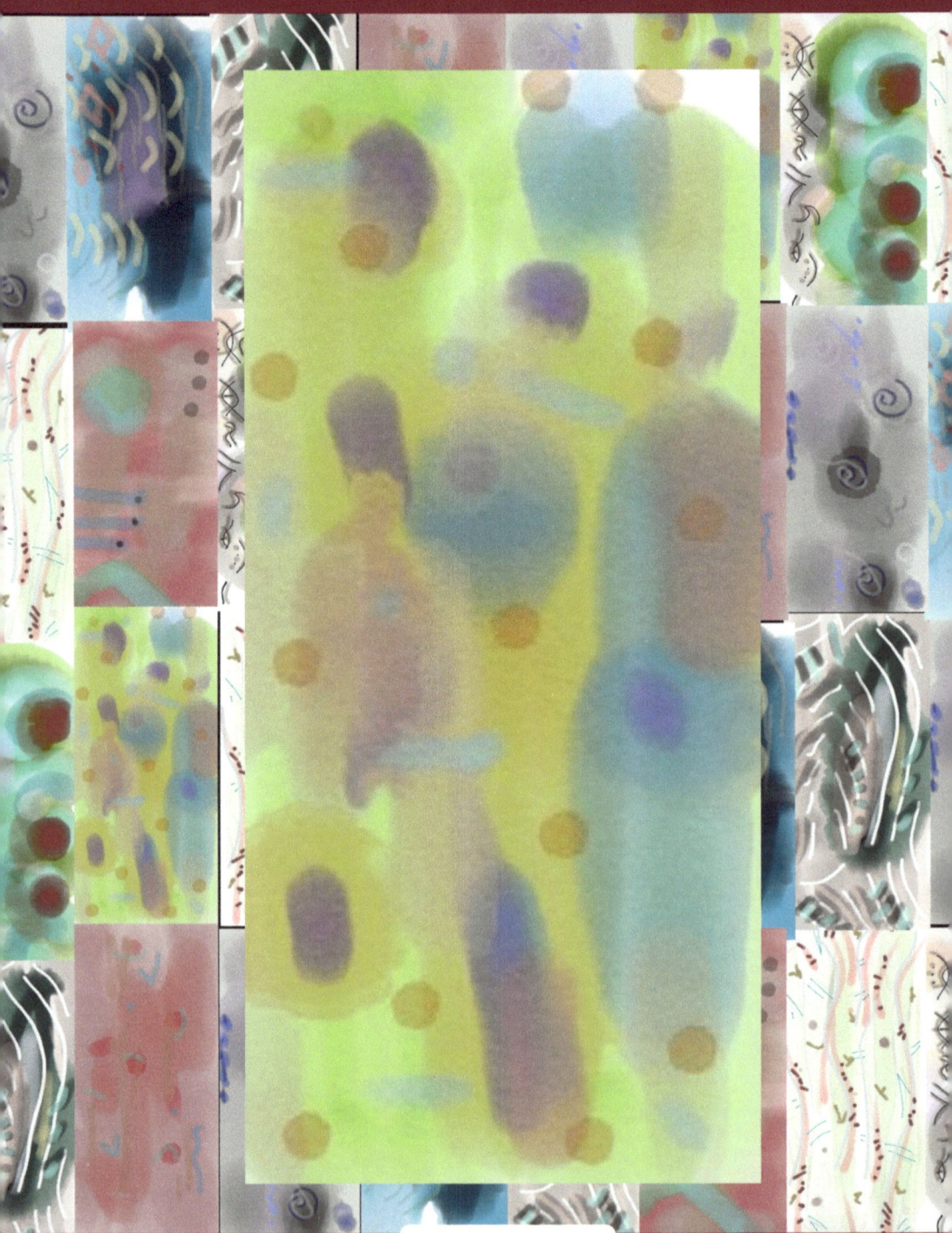

'Out of Focus'

Silent Talking: My Kundalini Nightmare

After many years of my try to recon with and understand, while listening to their lives in Hollywood reports—I felt I couldn't let them break her heart this far and I began to shut their 'calls' off. This was a new period of regaining strength for me, about fifteen years after my nightmare began. That soul muscle ability to shut a spirit transmission off grew strong. I felt like I was a radio and each entity transmitted through me on what felt like a different radio channel. I found I could turn a channel off with my own 'will' and stop their 'call'. I felt guilty I had this ability even though now I decided it was the right thing to do. Oddly she showed no signs of heartbreak one way or the other. My heart seemed to be breaking for her in empathy, but I saw no emotion from her at all. I also feared my channeling abilities created an electricity that could be keeping her ill and was shouting from time to time that we must stop 'call'. Her response was, "Don't yell at me!". That always shocked me. It wasn't the first time she ignored my subject and only addressed my tone.

 In hindsight, we perpetually never had enough food. I was starving beyond anorexic. I am now considering how under-nourishment could have even been a strong contributor to the causes of my nightmare kundalini event as well. At times we lived in a car as I had discussed, but before the 2000's from 1986 - 2000 we had had no bed.

I was guilty for those years, when we could never afford a new bed, because I was the one that failed at holding my bladder and peed in the bed. She always could succeed at the immensely agonizing years of living through her demand to hold it in. She named it 'wash pain'. I would sleep on the arm of a lounge chair and give her the chair. I again felt deserving of the punishment because I failed at twenty-four hour bladder holding. The only way I ever got through it not to continuously repeat the bed scenario was to literally only drink a couple sips of water a day. She on the other hand would gulp down glass after glass and could always hold it in. She prided herself on that one. The OCD premise, and it started in regards to her angel children, was that in order to protect them—we could not empty our bowels or bladder until the faucet sound in the pipes in the walls went silent. This must have been the use of others in the apartment building or a hose that was left on a tinkle. I would have to sit next to her in the agony of holding it in—clamping my muscle as the waves of pain came and subsided, came and subsided. The clock never seemed to move forward as the whole night would pass—second by second. The faucet sound was always there. When it started every night around ten pm, we must freeze and not move. My bladder would fill usually in about half an hour after freezing—it was tortuous by seven or eight am. We weren't allowed to fall asleep through the ritual. Sleep time was only after the sound stopped. The twenty-four hour episodes were also when we were on the road and she wouldn't let me stop until she said. It was usually once in twenty-four hours. At that point she was boasting that her 'wash pain' had gone away, that she had mastered it. Mine had not! Eventually I had more strength and I would pull the car off the freeway and find a toilet. Then I would be in massive guilt because she refused to 'go', even if I begged her. Over all the years, she would always come 'out of the blue' with another shocking practice for an impossible reason for the sake of protecting her angel children, and I to my dread would have to live through it. When I learned to refuse to drink fluids to survive the 'holding in wash pain' practice, in her mania she would scream at me to drink more—never acknowledging that her rituals were the reason I was adapting in this manner. The days she forced me to drink the full glass were torture.

At times we lived with her grandparents, at times with her mother—after we lost the apartment (more on that later). Strangely, neither her mother or grandparents ever provided us with a new bed after I ruined the original one. The bed I am referring to was the only one she ever had. The one that was in her room when we met and we moved it to the North Hollywood apartment in the beginning.

That was when and where the kundalini nightmare entrapped me and her OCD rituals came into play. As I mentioned there were MANY OCD rituals. I had to somehow endure them the very best I could because she had insisted that the well being of her angel children spirits depended on it. Later down the line, after she had declared that they were all famous actresses in Hollywood —it was then my responsibility not to fail at the rituals or something terrible might happen to these people. If it did— I could never live with myself. Some rituals she did alone and I was to stand still for hours watching her and she demanded I not flinch or move an inch until she succeeded. If I did, she would blame me that she had to start all over. This one went on for years. Over the years the rituals would run their course and that was a great blessing for me. At times though her demands were no less than, if I may say so now looking back, psychotic. She would have fits. Once she demanded I bring her an ice cream shake exactly at the minute on her birthday when she was born. If the ice cream was a fraction too melted for her specific liking, she would throw it all over the carpet and make me clean it up and then start over. Sometimes we went through this when it wasn't her birthday. There were dozens and dozens of these episodes about all kinds of subjects that I went through with her. I noted she was in her thirties at the time of this one and this is while she is calling herself 'The Angel of Truth', 'The Light of Truth', The only soul that can declare the 'Truth'. One of the episodes that deeply haunts me is when 'out of the blue' she starts screaming and demanding me to put my hand on the electric coil burner in the kitchen when it was on. "My hand?" "You want me to burn myself?" She answered, "Yes". I began to walk to the kitchen and then turned around and said I couldn't. She proceeded to scream at me for a full half an hour to "do it" as I stood there frozen. I realized to myself that it was a test of my love for her greatness and I gave in and burned my whole palm on the burner as she had asked. I shocked myself that I did it and returned with an entire coil mark burned into my skin. This was a simultaneous theme, that alongside the OCD rituals that were always physically painful and abusive, but with purpose, some were just because it's what she wanted—psychotically and sadistically wanted.

Back in the 1980's we lost the apartment when she refused to let me work (holy hands) and made me leave the jobs I had at the time. Her grandparents came and took us to their house. Both her mother and grandparents rented and moved about often and we lived like gypsies focused on the 'other side' and spiritual truths instead of reality. Remember, I had lost all agency over my life and all of these decisions and outcomes sickened and panicked me.

At some point I determined to myself, that surely one of her lovers or angel children who 'called' for so many years would know her when they saw her, since she now had her revelation and recognized the 'people' they were in the world. My next mission was to get her into Hollywood and famous enough to meet them. I suggested she write another movie, less expensive to sell. Possibly I thought to myself, she could meet her angel children/ actresses by casting them in her screenplay, if we could sell the movie. I had to succeed at finding the right health program to heal her by that time as well. I tried to stay focused and positive, I was determined to succeed for her health and happiness. I also felt urgency and desperate to get her to them, now that she realized they were living people, because I was exhausted from being 'call'. She wrote a romantic comedy ghost story and it was wonderful. It would be a low budget to produce and was an easier 'sell' because the subject was popular and very entertaining. Then I suggested she write her incredible truths in a book if we couldn't sell the Sci-Fi movie, so they wouldn't be lost. She wrote an astounding book. It was years of attempts and failure. Later on, she proceeded to paint amazing artwork and I bought her a synthesizer. She had insisted over the years to save one hundred dollars a month and put it away for HERSELF, even if we starved. This was around a time when we settled on a town and rented an apartment. That was of course the months her mother deposited a bit more than other times. Her mother would begin to make money and then always crashed her check amount by offending people and losing her 'group members' in a multi-level marketing business. This pattern of some money and then nothing repeated itself all the years. I was at the mercy of her and her mother (long story). The focus was so intensely on her evil mother as she perceived it, that I could never focus on her as anything else but the victim. With the synthesizer, she composed beautiful songs and music albums naturally with no training. Her college major was in social psychology. They rejected her entrance into the film department where she had applied first. I always found that perplexing. She had a beautiful singing voice and a natural talent to compose amazing music as well as write profoundly and paint lovely contemporary art. I can see I am putting my readers under her spell.

Silent Talking: My Kundalini Nightmare

'Ascending with Dove'

I had always imagined that one of these days she would be united with her 'soul family' as she had called it. I imagined her happy with all the people she had mentioned, health restored—and I, kind of alone—discarded because my only place was to be used for 'call', but at peace with that she was finally happy.

But that was never going to be the case. She passed in 2014, not without me bearing her body falling into complete devastation, tending to wounds and wounds and septic fevers and the terror of if she would make it and flies laying maggots in the wounds and taking out the worms, and staying up all night to catch the hidden fly that got in, so it wouldn't happen again. The more I regained my body and voice, and closed most of the 'calls', the more health emergencies and horrifying illness events, so gruesome I can't shake the memories. She passed in a hospital after all, not without the surgeon removing most of her intestines, the nurses saying it was the worst smell they ever smelled, I know, I went through trying to save her and washing out the only two pairs of underwear we could afford from the 'runs' day and night. Finally abdomen pain took over and she asked me for the first time in thirty years to take her to the hospital. I thought surely there had to be a miracle and it had to be 'now'—for she was the 'Light of Truth'.

I felt I failed her. I couldn't save her. She succumbed to an inevitable death. I said to myself, at least my efforts postponed it. I hated myself for being alive at that moment. Why was the better person dead? I spent the next three years self publishing her books, music albums and doing art shows in her memory to try to make up for it. I succeeded and even published a book about her being a victim to Dental Mercury Amalgam poisoning and how a great artist was lost. I achieved an entire radio station on Spotify in her memory with all her music and streamed her albums on music platforms across the world. It was my way to justify remaining alive and part of my process of mourning her. I was incredibly driven and her mother gave me some living expenses in trade for me publishing her work and keeping her memory alive. I had a job at the same time as well. I did all of this from a public library computer. Her mother paid for a hotel room for me to stay in that was near her grave and eventually I found a room to rent that was close to a public library. After three years I was really confused that even though I got good local feedback, nothing as great as her book of the truth, incredible poetry, photography and even a book of her art that was outstanding, took off. The same as a stopper on it all no matter how much I tried, as her movies before and saving her life most all.

Silent Talking: My Kundalini Nightmare

'Accelerating Circles'

10

Accelerating Forward

Accelerating forward nine and a half years later, I began to be reached and realized for the first time, she was a terrible person and abused me greatly. That I must unpublish and let all her incredible work go. I must bury it all with her, because whatever realm she pulled her greatness from, she wasn't deserving of. I had a talk with her mother who was her mortal enemy in her mind. Even though her mother deposited funds for her, she refused to speak to her at all. I finally realized her mother might not be the bad one after all and I told her mother the horrors her daughter put me through to some extent. The first I ever could tell anything to anyone. I was so brainwashed to keep her privacy and that meant to keep my own suffering private as well—even this long after her passing. What she said next was the greatest healing moment imaginable for me and shocked me completely.

Silent Talking: My Kundalini Nightmare

'I Finally See'

I explained to her that for myself it was a friendship, but for her it was…… and that I hadn't had sex since I was twenty-one before she had met me. I also got to finally explain to her much of what I have written here and she went into shock and told me she knew her daughter was disturbed, but couldn't have imagined this far, and that she thought our friendship was good.

Now she said she understood why her daughter died and I lived. It was so I could have a chance at life. The chance her daughter took.

That turned absolutely everything around. I began to see my way out. I began to be able to look back without guilt and realize—"I am abused". That it's now my journey to find myself again. My journey to recovery. There have been very slow ups and downs with amazing breakthroughs and feelings.

Silent Talking: My Kundalini Nightmare

'Ups & Downs'

11

SILENCE AND TOTALLY ALONE

Dear readers, that is one tenth the story quickly braised. Please note that her name is missing in my memoir because I have not yet been able to bear writing it down—nor showing any photos of her as well. As her body is bagged life becomes silent. At that moment of silence, I faced utter aloneness. My father had passed before I was twenty-one and my mother and only brother had passed during my thirty years of darkness and complete isolation with my kryptonite in human form. I had no children or communication with anyone else during those years. It was demanded I leave communication with my mother very early on, or they would leave me. It goes on and horribly on, and so complicated at that. My relationship with my only brother was lost due to the circumstances as well. Now in the stillness I must come out into the world, jump into finding a way to support myself at minimum wage and find myself again. I was in shock. The world and working was so noisy. I was falling into normalcy with my traumas buried inside. It was surreal. Everyone meeting me assumed my life was normal and I had to leave it at that.

Silent Talking: My Kundalini Nightmare

As a server in required attire, proceeding as if I belong, but feeling out of place and surreal to be back in the world like a 'first job' teenage newbie.

Becoming an artist was a calling. First I was inspired by Celtic tattoo designs and drawn to copper as my medium. I began to look for alternatives to enameling copper because it is so toxic and discovered tooling as in leather, then pewter. I decided, why not tool copper instead. Repoussé techniques really interested me but European works and old Americana Copper Relief Repoussé pieces came heavy handed, dark, ominous and depressing. I decided to tool mandalas of my design with a lighter style in copper and opened my Etsy shop 'CopperTattoo' (etsy.com/shop/coppertattoo). I have displayed and sold my Copper Repoussé pieces in galleries and at art festivals as well, but unfortunately the process became too labor intensive—causing hand pain, and the price of copper became too expensive to make more pieces.

Silent Talking: My Kundalini Nightmare

Copper Repoussé in Moss Patina - Tribal Mandala Series

Then I began getting more emotionally radical with graphic design artworks, and I am working on a new photo art greeting card line. It's fantasy art photography as well as visual art on greeting cards and canvas prints. I am a member of an artists association and display my canvas prints at the airport. I am also working on revising a very serious and beautiful book of original mandalas about the collective consciousness and healing through art inspired by sacred geometry. It will have mantras and mandalas to help guide your meditations. adriabooks.com

Silent Talking: My Kundalini Nightmare

'Dreams & Fire' Fantasy Photography

Silent Talking: My Kundalini Nightmare

'Succulent Bouquet Rose & Vase' Art Photography'

Trying to find the courage to express myself to create artwork was terrifying. After all, the best artist had passed and I couldn't possibly compare. I have discovered through taking the steps that my artwork truly comes out 'me' and it has helped lead me back to my original self to look at what I create. It's been part of my healing and helped me get to know myself again.

I hope that sharing my journey can help you realize that no matter what you are facing, there is a way to find—to help. My message to you the reader is don't give up. I think on all our life journeys we will meet and face our 'kryptonite' whether in chemical form, human form or something else even. Our challenge is to persevere and grow through it all and find ourselves again. Sharing our journey as well I believe helps us all get through.

Good luck, courage and strength to you for your life journey. I hope my tale and SILENT TALKING can help.

Sincerely, the Author & Artist *Adria Chalfin*

Silent Talking: My Kundalini Nightmare

To this very day the mystery of my channeling nightmare remains in the darkness. I have not encountered anyone that can explain it or reveal it to me. I have read books about channelers in the past and they go unconscious when the entity takes over. I am the first I have heard of that remained conscious and experienced a life event so cult-like and sexually orientated. I feel used and greatly traumatized still at this very moment but have gained strength, courage and excitement for life again.

Silent Talking: My Kundalini Nightmare

Me at seventeen as a member of the Heritage Dance Company- L.A.

Silent Talking: My Kundalini Nightmare

'Stoic Silent Talking' Visual Art Collage. Individual artworks inlayed into this collage are individually featured in this book. Each graphic design artwork, albeit radical, expresses the emotions I lived through when incapable to speak.

Silent Talking: My Kundalini Nightmare

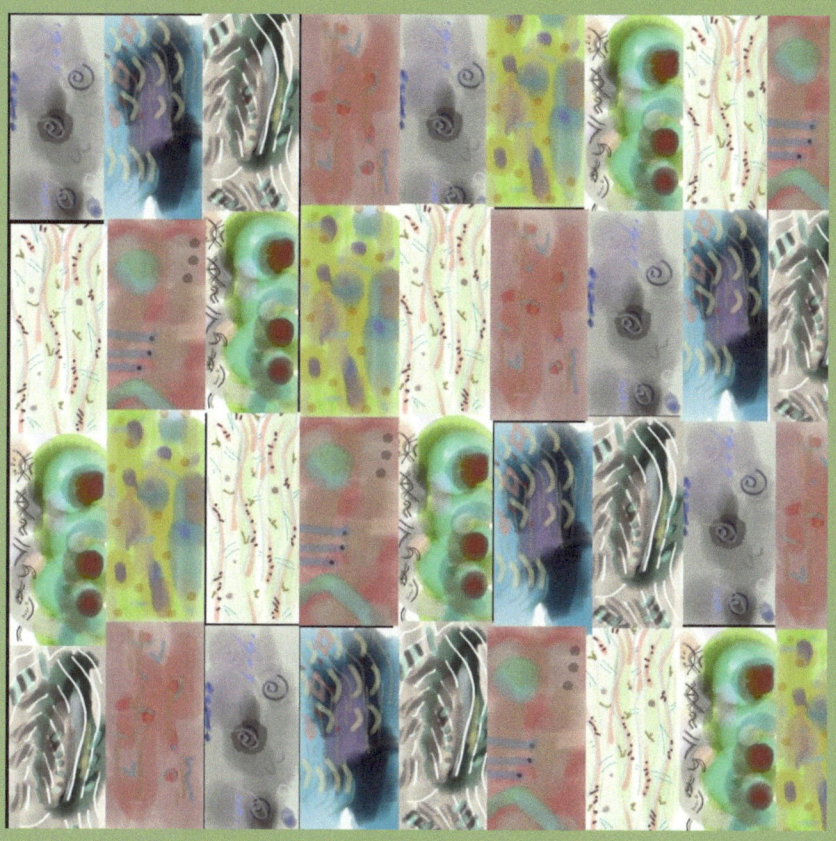

'Poetry' Visual Art Collage. Individual artworks inlayed into this collage are individually featured in this book, Each graphic design watercolor artwork, expresses a poem of thoughts and feelings expressed as art versus words.

Silent Talking: My Kundalini Nightmare

adriabooks.com

PO BOX 602
LOS ALAMOS CA
93440

www.ingramcontent.com/pod-product-compliance
Lightning Source LLC
Chambersburg PA
CBHW040440040426
42333CB00033B/68